M257 Unit 6
UNDERGRADUATE COMPUTING

Putting Java to work

Graphical user interfaces

Unit 6

This publication forms part of an Open University course M257 *Putting Java to work*. Details of this and other Open University courses can be obtained from the Student Registration and Enquiry Service, The Open University, PO Box 197, Milton Keynes MK7 6BJ, United Kingdom: tel. +44 (0)870 333 4340, email general-enquiries@open.ac.uk

Alternatively, you may visit the Open University website at http://www.open.ac.uk where you can learn more about the wide range of courses and packs offered at all levels by The Open University.

To purchase a selection of Open University course materials visit http://www.ouw.co.uk, or contact Open University Worldwide, Michael Young Building, Walton Hall, Milton Keynes MK7 6AA, United Kingdom for a brochure. tel. +44 (0)1908 858785; fax +44 (0)1908 858787; email ouwenq@open.ac.uk

The Open University
Walton Hall, Milton Keynes
MK7 6AA

First published 2007. Second edition 2008.

Edited, designed and typeset by The Open University.

Printed and bound in the United Kingdom by Hobbs the Printers Ltd.

ISBN 978 0 7492 6801 5

2.1

The paper used in this publication contains pulp sourced from forests independently certified to the Forest Stewardship Council® (FSC®) principles and criteria. Chain of custody certification allows the pulp from these forests to be tracked to the end use (see www.fsc-uk.org).

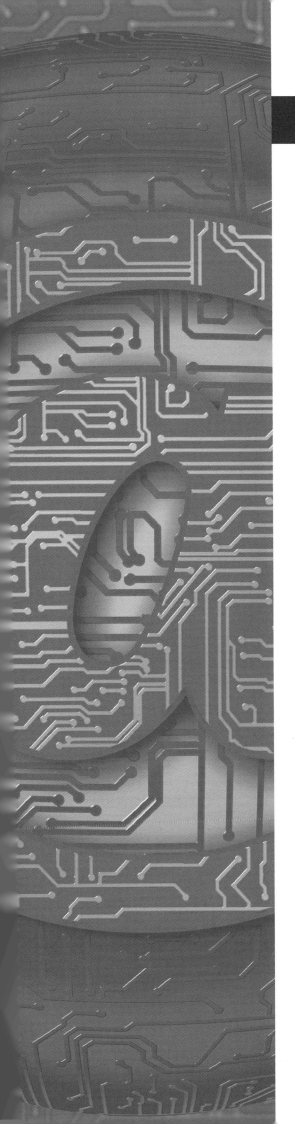

CONTENTS

M257 COURSE TEAM

M257 *Putting Java to work* was adapted from M254 *Java everywhere*.

M254 was produced by the following team.

Martin Smith, Course Team Chair and Author

Anton Dil, Author

Brendan Quinn, Author

Janet Van der Linden, Academic Editor

Barbara Poniatowska, Course Manager

Ralph Greenwell, Course Manager

Alkis Stavrinides, External Assessor, Coventry University

Critical readers

Pauline Curtis, Associate Lecturer

David Knowles, Associate Lecturer

Robin Walker, Associate Lecturer

Richard Walker, Associate Lecturer

The M257 adaptation was produced by:

Darrel Ince, Course Team Chair and Author

Richard Walker, Consultant Author and Critical Reader

Matthew Nelson, Critical Reader

Barbara Poniatowska, Course Manager

Ralph Greenwell, Course Manager

Alkis Stavrinides, External Assessor, Coventry University

Media development staff

Andrew Seddon, Media Project Manager

Garry Hammond, Editor

Ian Blackham, Editor

Anna Edgley-Smith, Editor

Jenny Brown, Freelance Editor

Andrew Whitehead, Designer and Graphic Artist

Glen Derby, Designer

Phillip Howe, Compositor

Lisa Hale, Compositor

Thanks are due to the Desktop Publishing Unit of the Faculty of Mathematics and Computing.

1 Introduction

In the previous unit we described how data such as that from a file could be communicated to a Java program. However, there is also a need to handle data that is communicated in more diverse fashions and, in particular, directly from a human. Such data is often taken into a system via a **graphical user interface** (GUI). GUI design is a major field of study and creating a 'usable' interface is crucial to the development of a successful software system. The interfaces that you will create in this course will be relatively simple and will not require a great deal of planning and design. However, for commercial systems, a substantial amount of time and effort is required to ensure that the interface presented to the user enables easy and indeed enjoyable interaction. Typically, these interfaces will include buttons, areas for typing in text, drop-down menus for selecting options, areas for displaying results, and so on. These are known as visual components.

In this unit, we will look at how such interfaces can be created and displayed. The next unit will show how we can then get such interfaces to respond to the user interacting with them.

In this unit, we aim to:

► introduce graphical user interfaces (GUI);

► present a range of visual components;

► show how components can be placed to create an interface;

► give you an overall view of the construction of a working GUI.

2 Overview of the Swing library

The part of the Java system that contains classes that enable less structured information to be input and output is known as the **Swing** library. It contains pre-built classes of graphical interface elements. While it is possible to build an interface from scratch using the basic drawing primitives (rectangle, line, text) you will, for simplicity and consistency, mainly rely on the tools that the Java language provides.

As with other parts of this course, we do not aim to provide a fully comprehensive coverage of all of the Swing classes. There are numerous Swing classes, which contain many methods, but this unit will provide you with enough knowledge and experience to use the `javax.swing` class library and other related libraries.

The Swing library is an extension of Java's Abstract Windowing Toolkit (AWT). The AWT is the part of the Java run-time system that is responsible for user interaction with window objects. The AWT does have its own set of visual components but, among other things, they suffer from the disadvantage of not looking the same on all platforms. This is due to the display of the components being closely tied to the underlying operating system. In this course, we will make use of components from the Swing library only, although we will need to import parts of the underlying AWT library.

The Swing library components look the same on every platform and so you do not have to worry about any inconsistencies between platforms. Unlike the AWT components, Swing components are not so closely tied to the underlying operating system.

Swing can be broken down into groups of related classes. In this section, we will make a quick tour of each of the following groups and then return to them later by describing some small examples that illustrate them.

▶ **Containers**. A container is a component that can hold other components. Among the containers provided by Swing we will use two in particular; these are `JFrame` and `JPanel`. The class `JFrame` maintains a `Container` called the content pane. This contains all of the visual components, including other containers such as `JPanel`, through which the user interacts with the computer program. A **panel** groups elements in an area of a window and is then added to a `JFrame` component.

▶ **Layout managers**. These are used with containers to arrange embedded components into a particular layout style; for example, laying the components out in a grid. The various layout managers are used to ensure consistent spacing or alignment and include `BorderLayout`, `FlowLayout`, `GridLayout`, `GridBagLayout` and `BoxLayout`. You will meet a number of these in this unit.

▶ **Visual components**. This group of components provides the means by which users will usually interact with your applications. They include controls such as buttons. They form the backbone of the Swing library and will be the building blocks of most Java applications that require user interfaces.

An important part of the `Swing` hierarchy is shown in Figure 1.

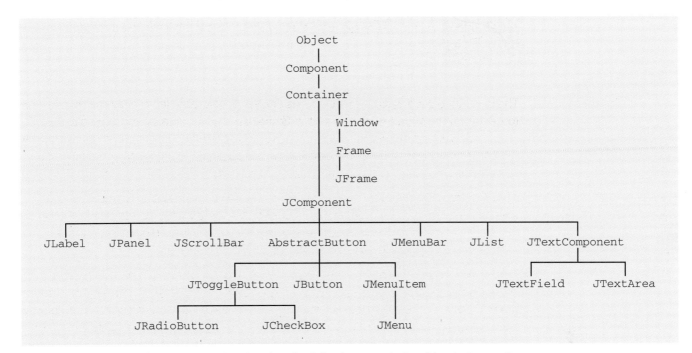

Figure 1   Part of the Swing hierarchy showing the inheritance relationships between the various Swing components and, ultimately, `Object`

The `Swing` library classes have class names that start with a `J`, such as `JButton` or `JMenuBar`. An exception is `AbstractButton`, which is part of Swing, but doesn't start with a `J`. As this diagram shows, the Swing components inherit a great deal of their methods and behaviours from other classes. When you use the Java API library to look up methods and behaviours of components, you should also look at the classes from which a component inherits.

There are a number of aspects to programming an interface:

1   the GUI components that you use;

2   the way that these components are laid out on a screen;

3   the way that the program that uses the interface responds to events that occur with an interface, such as a mouse being clicked or text being entered into a text field.

We begin in Section 3 by looking at how visual components can be arranged within containers and within a frame on screen using various layout managers. We will use the button as an example of a familiar visual component to illustrate these issues.

In Section 4 we look at some of the many other GUI visual components available in the Swing library.

In Section 5, we put the ideas from Sections 3 and 4 together and also introduce additional components. This section also illustrates the use of inheritance and polymorphism in building complex user interfaces.

The third aspect listed above, that of getting the program to respond to button clicks, menu selections and so on, involves the very important subject of **event-driven programming**, which is the main subject of *Unit 7.*

Calculator interface

In order to illustrate the construction of a GUI in the following sections, we will look at the design and development of a simple calculator interface. The completed GUI is shown in Figure 2.

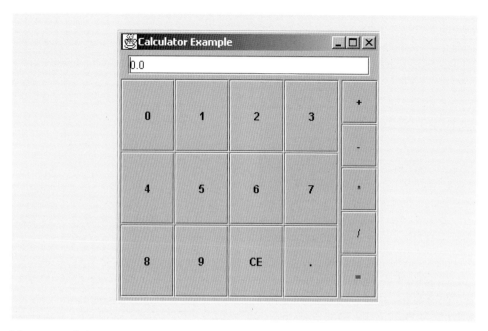

Figure 2   Calculator interface showing number and function buttons with a display for output

The functionality of the calculator has been kept simple in order to focus on the approach to constructing a GUI. Similarly, the style of the components used has been kept simple. This calculator allows the user to use the buttons to enter a real number, which is displayed in the space at the top. The user can then select a function and click on the = button to see the result. The CE button allows the user to clear the entries and start again.

The complete code for the calculator is given in Appendix 1 at the end of this unit. On completion of this unit you will understand how the graphical interface is constructed. Getting the graphical interface to respond to the user is the subject of the next unit, so we will continue working on this example in *Unit 7*. As a result, there will be some parts of the code that you will not understand at the end of this unit but all will become clear at the end of *Unit 7*.

3 Containers and layouts

We will start by looking at how visual components are placed in a component known as a container. Later on in this section we shall look at how to create a button so that we can use it as an example of a visual component to illustrate various layouts.

In this course, you will meet three containers and these are as follows.

▶ JFrame. This is a window used in Java applications.

▶ JApplet. This is a container that can be embedded in a web page (applets will be considered in another unit).

▶ JPanel. This is a container that can be used in both applications and applets. Panels, like all containers, can contain both visual components and other containers. You will find yourself using instances of the JPanel class very frequently as they provide a large amount of flexibility in laying out visual components.

The container JFrame represents an application window that is represented on a display device and with which the user can interact. A JFrame is able to nest (contain) other components. The actual elements in the JFrame are held in its content pane, which is the usable area of the frame in which other components can be placed. It does not include the title bar along the top of the frame containing the 'coffee cup' icon (or any other icon that the programmer chooses – see the Java API documentation if you wish to follow this up), the title of the frame (again set by the programmer) and the standard window buttons.

The interface for an application is usually created by inheriting from JFrame. This allows the application to inherit all of the non-private methods within JFrame. There are many inherited methods but we will look at the most commonly used ones, as listed in Table 1.

Table 1   Methods of class JFrame

Method signature	Description
setLayout(LayoutManager)	sets a particular style of layout
add(Component)	includes a component
remove(Component)	removes a component
setVisible(boolean)	makes the window visible or not
setTitle(String)	gives the window a title
getContentPane()	gets access to the content pane

As you will see later, many of these methods are also used with JPanel. A panel is a container that can contain other containers and also GUI visual components such as buttons. Thus panels allow you to modularize the layout of the GUI. A frame is a window in which containers (such as panels) and visual components (such as buttons) can be embedded. These correspond to the normal windows you see when using an operating system such as Windows.

The way in which visual components are laid out inside a container depends on the way you specify its layout. In order for you to communicate your requirements, layout managers provide a number of patterns that you can adopt.

Each container has a method called `setLayout`, which allows you to specify the pattern of layout for the visual components within the container. There are a number of standard layout patterns that can be set for a container but each type of container has a default pattern. The container `JFrame` has a default pattern of `BorderLayout` and `JPanel` has a default of `FlowLayout`.

At this stage, do not worry about what the `BorderLayout` or the `FlowLayout` does; all you need to know is that the code says that when you add components they will obey the `BorderLayout` rules or the `FlowLayout` rules. We shall discuss the various layouts later in this unit.

We will give a series of code fragments or small applications to cover specific topics. We won't cover every element in the Swing library, but there will be enough to give you a solid foundation and allow you to access the Swing library with confidence. When you start to use the Swing classes you will almost certainly begin to develop your own personal style of writing user interfaces but, until that happens, the most effective way to progress is to experiment liberally with the classes until you find something that you like and which solves the particular problem in hand.

We shall start by showing you how to create containers and then demonstrate some layout techniques.

3.1 Using containers

An object of class `Window` provides a top-level window without borders or a title bar. As it stands it is not entirely useful, except for implementing a pop-up window, but it forms the basic building unit for the `Window` subclasses. The `JFrame` subclass, for example, has borders and a title bar and is normally used as the root window for building stand-alone Java applications.

The following code is a very simple application that displays a frame and sets the title of the window:

```
import java.awt.*;
import javax.swing.*;

public class FrameDemo extends JFrame
{
    public FrameDemo (String title)
    {
        setSize(200, 200);
        setTitle(title);
    }
}
```

To run the code we use the following class:

```
public class FrameDemoTest
{
    public static void main (String[] args)
    {
        FrameDemo fd = new FrameDemo("We Love Java");
        fd.setVisible(true);
    }
}
```

Remember that a `JFrame` object is normally used for applications. The above code creates a frame, sizes the frame (to 200 by 200 pixels), sets the title and then displays it on the screen using the method `setVisible(true)`. Once you have an object that is described by a class that is a subclass of the `Container` class (for example, `JFrame`) then you can add other user interface elements quite easily. If you run the code for class `FrameDemoTest`, you will see a simple window on your screen. The screen shot corresponding to the code above is shown in Figure 3.

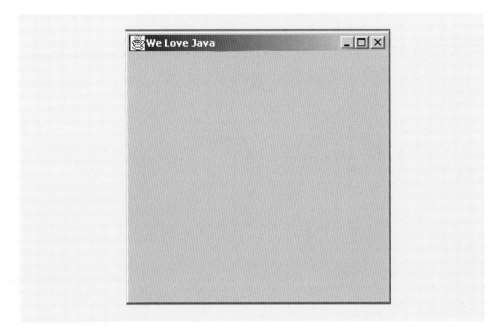

Figure 3   A simple frame showing only a title, the standard icon and the window buttons

If you press the close box in the top right-hand corner, the window disappears as you would expect. However, the program has not stopped running. In order to stop the program you will need to use the facilities of your IDE interface. You will see in *Unit 7* how to link clicking the close button on a window to actually stopping the program.

Once you have created a top-level frame you can use the `JPanel` class to divide it up into manageable sections.

3.2   Placing elements using `LayoutManager`

We will now extend our simple `FrameDemo` class in Subsection 3.1 to include more features. In particular, we will demonstrate some of the ways that instances of classes that implement the `LayoutManager` interface can be used to place elements automatically. Each class that implements `LayoutManager` can create layouts that will place elements according to some algorithm; for example, `BorderLayout` uses the points of the compass.

In order to illustrate the effects of the different layouts, we need to have a visual component that we can place in a frame or in a panel. Section 4 discusses a wide range of visual components but for now we will introduce how to use a **button**, in order to illustrate the effects of the layouts.

Buttons

Buttons are normally used in an interface to signify that some form of processing is to occur. A button, like every other Java element, is an object and is defined by a class within Swing. To create an unlabelled or labelled button you need to use new. For example, the statement:

```
JButton offButton = new JButton();
```

creates an unlabelled button, and:

```
JButton onButton = new JButton("Cancel");
```

creates a button with the label given by the string, which is its argument.

If you want to change the label on a button then you invoke the setText method. For example:

```
offButton.setText("Press Me");
```

would associate the label "Press Me" with the button offButton. To find the label associated with a button use the getText method. Thus:

```
String offButtonLabel = offButton.getText();
```

sets the string variable offButtonLabel to "Press Me".

We are now in a position to continue looking at layouts.

The **BorderLayout** class

We will start with the BorderLayout class. Our example code looks like this:

```
import java.awt.*;
import javax.swing.*;

public class FrameDemo extends JFrame
{
    private final int numOfBut = 5;
    private JButton[] buttons = new JButton[numOfBut];

    public FrameDemo (String title)
    {
        setSize(300, 300);
        setTitle(title);

        /* Create and name some buttons. */
        for (int i = 0; i < numOfBut; i++)
        {
            buttons[i] = new JButton("Button " + i);
        }

        /* Place some buttons. */
        Container cp = getContentPane();
        cp.add(buttons[0], BorderLayout.NORTH);
        cp.add(buttons[1], BorderLayout.SOUTH);
        cp.add(buttons[2], BorderLayout.EAST);
        cp.add(buttons[3], BorderLayout.WEST);
        cp.add(buttons[4], BorderLayout.CENTER);
    }
}
```

The code simply fleshes out the previous example for frames and can be tested using the class `FrameDemoTest` as given previously. We define an array of buttons, each of which is created with a numbered string. We have used the default layout for a `JFrame`, which is the `BorderLayout`. The method `getContentPane` gives us access to the container holding the window components. We then place each button into the content pane.

In fact, it is no longer necessary since Java 5 to invoke the methods `add` (and its variants), `remove` and `setLayout` on a content pane. Instead, they can be invoked directly on a `JFrame`, and will be invoked on its content pane behind the scenes. We have shown the earlier style here as you are still likely to encounter it in GUI code for some time to come and because it highlights the fact that these methods are actually being performed on a container within the `JFrame`.

When using the `BorderLayout` model each element is placed in the frame using a static constant `NORTH`, `EAST`, `SOUTH`, `WEST` and `CENTER`. These define where in the frame the objects are placed, following the rough basis of a compass (see Figure 4). When you add items to a container you always use an `add` method.

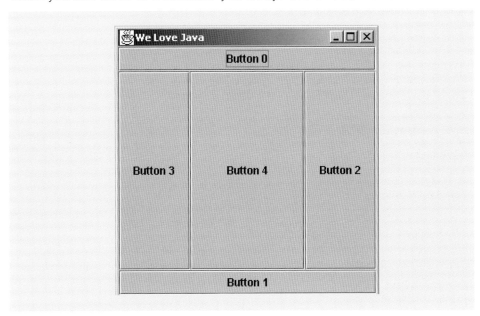

Figure 4   A border layout with five buttons

The element, which is placed at the `CENTER` (note the American spelling) location, is allocated as much space as has been left over by the other elements.

You can see how the elements are placed on the points of a compass. Notice that the two buttons placed into the frame at `NORTH` and `SOUTH` are expanded to fill the whole width of the frame.

The `BorderLayout` can also be used with other components, and not just with `JFrame`. Since `BorderLayout` is the default with `JFrame`, we can use it without having to set the layout style. If we want to use this style with a `JPanel` component we must explicitly request it.

```
JPanel p = new JPanel();
p.setLayout(new BorderLayout());
p.add(new JButton("press"), "North");
p.add(new JButton("reporter"), "South");
```

With `JPanel` there is no content pane to access to add or remove components. Note also that the strings `"North"`, `"South"` and so on are acceptable in place of constants such as `BorderLayout.NORTH`.

A panel is a container that can be used to group visual objects.

Activity 6.1
Constructing a frame with buttons, using `BorderLayout`.

The **FlowLayout** class

The next layout we will examine is FlowLayout. This is the default layout for JPanel, but has to be explicitly requested for JFrame. This layout places the items in the order in which they are added. If there isn't enough room on a line to include all of the components then they will flow onto the next line.

```java
public class FrameDemoTest
{
    public static void main (String[] args)
    {
        FrameDemo fd = new FrameDemo("We Love Java");
        fd.setVisible(true);
    }
}

import java.awt.*;
import javax.swing.*;

public class FrameDemo extends JFrame
{
    private final int numOfBut = 20;
    private JButton[] buttons = new JButton[numOfBut];

    public FrameDemo (String title)
    {
        setSize(300, 300);
        setTitle(title);

        /* Create some buttons. */
        for (int i = 0; i < numOfBut; i++)
        {
            buttons[i] = new JButton("Button " + i);
        }

        /* Place some buttons. */
        Container cp = getContentPane();
        cp.setLayout(new FlowLayout());
        for (int i = 0; i < numOfBut; i++)
        {
            cp.add(buttons[i]);
        }
    }
}
```

The resulting display is shown in Figure 5 (overleaf).

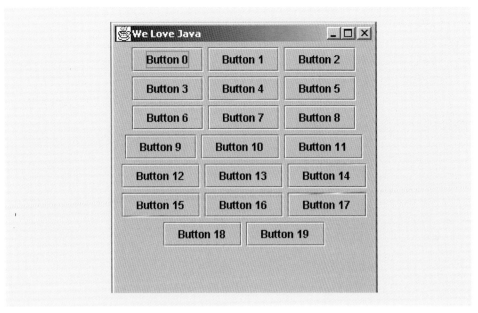

Figure 5   A flow layout with 20 buttons

The GridLayout class

The final layout we will describe here is the GridLayout class. What this layout does is to place the elements to be added according to a grid of rows and columns. When you define a GridLayout object it has two arguments: the first is the number of rows and the second is the number of columns. The code to demonstrate this is shown below; it uses three rows and two columns (see Figure 6).

```
import java.awt.*;
import javax.swing.*;

public class FrameDemo extends JFrame
{
    private final int numOfBut = 5;
    private JButton[] buttons = new JButton[numOfBut];

    public FrameDemo (String title)
    {
        setSize(300, 300);
        setTitle(title);

        /* Create some buttons. */
        for (int i = 0; i < numOfBut; i++)
        {
            buttons[i] = new JButton("Button " + i);
        }

        /* Place some buttons. */
        Container cp = getContentPane();
        // set size of grid - rows then columns
        cp.setLayout(new GridLayout(3, 2));
        for (int i = 0; i < numOfBut; i++)
        {
            cp.add(buttons[i]);
        }
    }
}
```

The display corresponding to the code is shown in Figure 6.

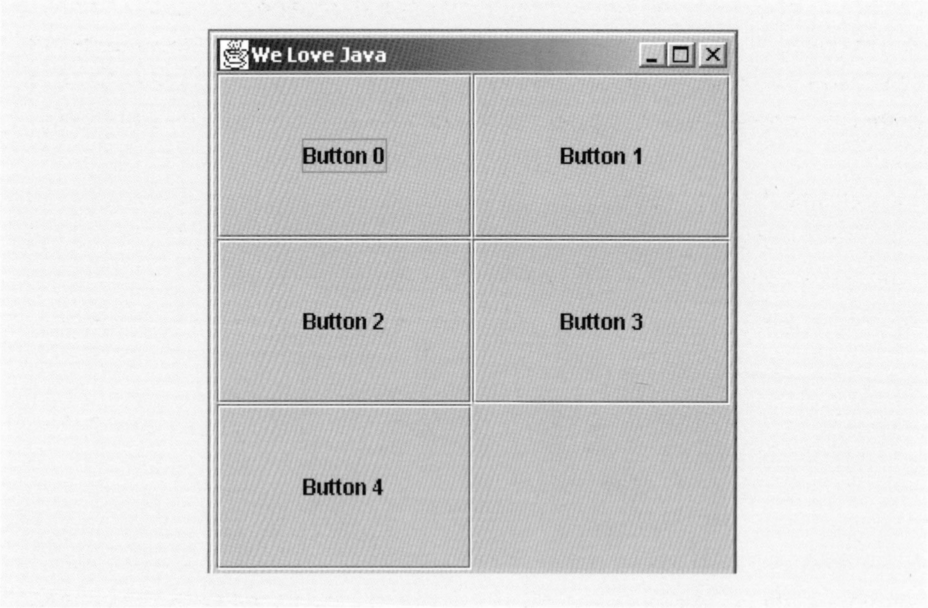

Activity 6.2
Constructing a frame
using `GridLayout`.

Figure 6   A grid layout with five buttons

As you might expect, in the `GridLayout` model the elements are arranged into a grid. Note how the grid is filled. Here five buttons have been added with the remaining part of the grid being empty.

We have explained just three of the standard layout models that are supported in Java. Among the other standard models are `CardLayout`, `GridBagLayout` and `BoxLayout`. The models are simple and easy to work with. In cases where the standard models do not meet your requirements, you can write some bespoke classes using the `LayoutManager` interface; however, the details of this are outside the scope of this course.

As an aside, it is worth mentioning that it is also possible not to use any layout manager and to place components manually. This is known as **absolute positioning**. It is done by specifying the layout manager to be `null`, adding the component to the holder in the normal way and then using the `setBounds` method to place and size the component in the holder. For example:

```
...
holder.setLayout(null);
JButton b1 = new JButton("Java!");
holder.add(b1);
b1.setBounds(10, 10, 20, 20);
...
```

The advantage of this is that you get greater control over placement. The disadvantage is that every element has to be placed manually, rather than relying on a layout manager. This can have major ramifications when you have to change the user interface; for example, inserting a new element will mean that many of the existing elements will need to be moved.

Calculator interface

You are now in a position to tackle the major part of the development of the calculator interface discussed in the previous section. The first step in the process is to decide what you would like the graphical interface to look like. We need the following items:

▶ something to present the results to the calculator user (a text field – see the next section);

▶ buttons for the digits 0 – 9;

▶ a button for the decimal point;

▶ buttons for the four basic functions (for this limited example);

▶ a button to force the results of the calculation to be displayed (an '=' button);

▶ a CE (clear entry) button.

There are many ways of setting out such a combination of components and Figure 2 shows only one of them.

SAQ 1

Activity 6.3
Simulating a control panel in a lift.

(a) The interface shown in Figure 2 is divided into a number of different areas. How many areas have been used and how can this be achieved?

(b) What is the advantage of dividing the interface in this way?

(c) Which layout managers have been used in each of the areas of the interface? Which layout manager would you use to arrange the panels into the frame?

ANSWERS ....

(a) This particular interface is divided into three areas. The simplest way is to make use of a number of panels to group the various components as follows:

▶ one panel for the text field;

▶ one for the digits, the decimal point and CE buttons;

▶ one for the function buttons, including the '=' button.

(b) By dividing the interface like this, we could use a different layout manager in each area to achieve a more complex interface than if we had only one layout manager for the whole interface.

(c) The text field panel has only one component and has simply used the default layout. The other two panels have used the grid layout. The panels were arranged in the frame using a border layout.

So, to summarize: to achieve this particular layout the visual components have been set out on three panels, one for the text field (the `displayPanel`), one for the digit buttons, tho point and the CE buttons using a grid layout of 3 × 4 (the `keyPadPanel`) and finally one for the function buttons and the equals button using a grid layout of 5 × 1 (the `functionPanel`). These three panels were then added to the frame using a border layout and the NORTH, CENTER and EAST positions. The part of the code that achieves this is given below. This section of code shows the declaration of the variables, followed by the constructor that creates the graphical interface.

```java
private final int NUMBER_KEY_PAD_BUTTONS = 10;
private final int NUMBER_DIGITS = 25;

private JButton [] keyPadButtons;
private JButton clearButton;
private JButton pointButton;
private JPanel keyPadPanel;
private JPanel displayPanel;
private JPanel functionPanel;
private JButton addButton;
private JButton subtractButton;
private JButton multiplyButton;
private JButton divideButton;
private JButton equalsButton;
private JTextField displayField;      // see Section 4

// four variables to handle the calculations
private String currentDisplay;
private String operand1;
private int function;
private double result;

public Calculator (String title)      // constructor
{
    setSize(300, 300);
    setTitle(title);
    currentDisplay = "";

    /* Set up key pad panel containing number, CE and
    point buttons.*/
    keyPadPanel = new JPanel();
    keyPadPanel.setLayout(new GridLayout(3, 4));
    keyPadButtons = new JButton[NUMBER_KEY_PAD_BUTTONS];

    /* Create each number button, add to panel
    and add action listener.*/
    for (int i = 0; i<NUMBER_KEY_PAD_BUTTONS; i++)
    {
        keyPadButtons[i]=new JButton("" + i);
        keyPadPanel.add(keyPadButtons[i]);
        keyPadButtons[i].addActionListener(new
            KeyPadButtonWatcher());        // see Unit 7
    }

    /* Create CE and point buttons, add to panel and add
    action listener.*/
    clearButton = new JButton("CE");
    pointButton = new JButton(".");
    keyPadPanel.add(clearButton);
    keyPadPanel.add(pointButton);
    clearButton.addActionListener(new
        KeyPadButtonWatcher());        // see Unit 7
    pointButton.addActionListener(new
        KeyPadButtonWatcher());        // see Unit 7
```

```
        // set up display field panel
        displayPanel = new JPanel();
        // see Section 4
        displayField = new JTextField(NUMBER_DIGITS);
        displayField.setText("0.0");
        displayPanel.add(displayField);

        // create function panel and function buttons
        functionPanel = new JPanel();
        functionPanel.setLayout(new GridLayout(5, 1));
        addButton = new JButton("+");
        subtractButton = new JButton("-");
        multiplyButton = new JButton("*");
        divideButton = new JButton("/");
        equalsButton = new JButton("=");

        // add function buttons to panel
        functionPanel.add(addButton);
        functionPanel.add(subtractButton);
        functionPanel.add(multiplyButton);
        functionPanel.add(divideButton);
        functionPanel.add(equalsButton);

        // add action listeners to function buttons - see Unit 7
        addButton.addActionListener(new
            FunctionButtonWatcher());
        subtractButton.addActionListener(new
            FunctionButtonWatcher());
        multiplyButton.addActionListener(new
            FunctionButtonWatcher());
        divideButton.addActionListener(new
            FunctionButtonWatcher());
        equalsButton.addActionListener(new
            EqualsButtonWatcher());

        // add functionality to close icon - see Unit 7
        setDefaultCloseOperation(JFrame.EXIT_ON_CLOSE);

        // get content pane and add panels to frame
        Container cp = getContentPane();
        cp.add(displayPanel,BorderLayout.NORTH);
        cp.add(keyPadPanel,BorderLayout.CENTER);
        cp.add(functionPanel,BorderLayout.EAST);
    }
```

Achieving a layout that is both aesthetically pleasing and easy for the user to use is part of a very large field of study known as human–computer interaction (HCI). The Java libraries contain many methods that will enable you to produce more sophisticated graphical interfaces than the one produced here. For example, it is possible to have buttons with bevelled edges, containing icons and so on, to enable you to produce professional graphical interfaces.

The rest of the calculator code is concerned with giving functionality to the buttons and we will study this in *Unit 7*.

SAQ 2

(a) What is the top-level window we will use in creating the interface for visual applications?

(b) How is a `JFrame` usually incorporated into an application?

(c) Which method of `JFrame` is used to display the frame and its contents on the screen?

ANSWERS ....

(a) All applications are held within a frame, which is created as an instance of a subclass of the `JFrame` class.

(b) Applications inherit from `JFrame` and so have access to the public and protected methods of `JFrame`.

(c) The method `setVisible` is used to display a frame and its contents.

4 GUI elements

The aim of this section is to examine some of the many visual components that you can place in containers. Section 3 showed you how to place buttons into frames and panels. The other visual components that you will meet in this section are placed in exactly the same way as buttons.

A note on naming: there is a potential for confusion arising when dealing with Swing components. Swing components begin with J – for example, JButton, JCheckBox. However, there are components, such as Button and Checkbox, that belong to the older AWT library. We will be dealing exclusively with Swing components in this course and so whenever you see button, check box and so on, we are talking about the Swing concept of a button, a check box and so on, and not the AWT components.

4.1 Buttons

You have already met the material in Subsection 3.2. However, we have repeated it here for completeness so that you have all of the information on the visual components in one place. A **button** is normally used in an interface to signify that some form of processing will occur. Like every other Java element, it is an object and is defined by a class within Swing. To create an unlabelled or labelled button you need to use new. For example, the statement:

A button is used so that the user can ask for action from a program.

```
JButton offButton = new JButton();
```

creates an unlabelled JButton, and:

```
JButton onButton = new JButton("Cancel");
```

creates a JButton with the label given by the constructor's argument.

An important point to make at this point is that the code above has not yet displayed the button on screen. It has just created a button object. The next section will show you how to display visual components.

If you want to change the label on a button then you invoke the setText method of a button. For example:

```
offButton.setText("Press Me");
```

associates the label "Press Me" with the button offButton. To find the label associated with a button use the getText method. Thus:

```
String offButtonLabel = offButton.getText();
```

sets the string variable offButtonLabel to "Press Me".

4.2 Labels

You can't do much with labels; they are just used for identifying more powerful visual objects.

A **label** is just text that can be placed within a container. To create a label, use `new`. For example:

```
JLabel headLb = new JLabel("Verbose Interface Cluster");
```

associates the reference `headLb` with the `JLabel` whose text is `"Verbose Interface Cluster"`. You can change the text associated with a label by using the method `setText` and you can retrieve the text associated with a label by using the method `getText`.

For example:

```
JLabel lb = new JLabel("Hello there");
...
lb.setText("Good Bye");
...
String currentLabelStr = lb.getText();
...
```

sets a label, then overwrites its text with a new string and, finally, sets the string `currentLabelStr` to the current string associated with the label.

4.3 Check boxes

Check boxes are used for the input of boolean data.

A **check box** is used to provide a `boolean` value for a program. For example, a check box may be used to indicate that the user is a novice or an experienced user.

As with all other visual components, check boxes are created using `new`. Two examples of this are shown below:

```
JCheckBox noviceUserType = new JCheckBox("Novice");
JCheckBox expeUserType = new JCheckBox("Experienced");
```

Check boxes can be either on or off, depending on whether or not they have been clicked. The state of a check box – whether or not it has been clicked – can be discovered by means of the method `isSelected`, which returns a `boolean` result. Thus:

```
boolean b = expeUserType.isSelected();
```

will place `true` or `false` in b depending on whether or not a user has clicked the check box.

4.4 Radio buttons

Radio buttons allow the user to choose one of a list of choices. The name comes from the idea of the preset station buttons on a radio – you can select only one station at any one time.

A special type of button is the **radio button**. Radio buttons are grouped together and have the property that only one of the buttons can be selected at a time. Clicking on a radio button means that the radio button that was selected previously becomes unselected.

Radio buttons are created using the class `JRadioButton` and are grouped together in a `ButtonGroup`. The code that illustrates this is shown below:

```
// first create the button group
ButtonGroup language = new ButtonGroup();
...
// then create the buttons
JRadioButton frenchButton =
    new JRadioButton("French", true);
JRadioButton germanButton =
    new JRadioButton("German", false);
JRadioButton englishButton =
    new JRadioButton("English", false);
...
// then add the buttons to the button group
language.add(frenchButton);
language.add(germanButton);
language.add(englishButton);
...
```

In the code, a `ButtonGroup` object is first created and then three `JRadioButtons` are created using the two-argument constructor for that class. The first argument is the label for the radio button and the second argument is a boolean that indicates how the radio button is initially set. In this case, the `"French"` button will be selected initially.

The `ButtonGroup` links the radio buttons together logically so that only one can be selected at any time, but it does not display the radio buttons visually. In order to see the radio buttons you will have to add them to a `JPanel` and then cause the `JPanel` to be displayed. This also aids in placing the whole group of radio buttons on the screen as a coherent group.

4.5 | Combo boxes (drop-down lists)

A **combo box** is a **drop-down list** that allows the programmer to specify a number of strings, one of which can be selected. Like the radio buttons, it is a way to force the user to select only one of the options offered. The code for creating a drop-down list is shown below:

Combo boxes are normally used when the user is required to choose from a large number of options or where the list of options changes dynamically.

```
JComboBox computerChoice = new JComboBox();
computerChoice.addItem("VAX");
computerChoice.addItem("PC");
computerChoice.addItem("Mac");
computerChoice.setSelectedItem("VAX");
```

The first line creates the drop-down list. The next three lines add three strings to the list and the final line sets the first string to be displayed. When the user clicks on the menu all three strings will be displayed and one can be selected.

As with all of the Swing classes there are many methods associated with this class. The most important one is `getSelectedItem`, which returns the string of the currently selected item. So, for example, the code:

```
String currentChoice = computerChoice.getSelectedItem();
```

results in the string `currentChoice` being set to the string `"VAX"`.

4.6 | Lists

The `JList` component is different from the drop-down list in the previous section. Whereas the `JComboBox` drops down when activated, the `JList` component occupies a fixed number of lines. The user can select a single string or a number of strings.

The simplest way to create a **list** is first to create an array containing the choices available and then to pass this array to the `JList` constructor.

```
String [] data = {"brendan", "anton", "barbara", "martin"};
JList nameList = new JList(data);
```

We can now use `nameList` to reference the list of names.

There are a number of methods that can be used to modify items in a list and to select the items that have been clicked. Some of the more important ones are described below:

▶ `public Object[] getSelectedValues()` returns an array of `Object` that contains references to the items that have been selected. For example, the code:

```
Object [] selectedNames = nameList.getSelectedValues();
```

places references to the `data` array strings that have been selected by the user into the `Object` array `selectedNames`.

▶ `public int[] getSelectedIndices()` returns an array of all the selected indices in increasing order.

If you retrieve the `ListModel` for a `JList`, using `getModel()`, you can also identify the object at each index of the `JList`, for example you can retrieve the string at index 1 of the `nameList` as follows:

```
nameList.getModel().getElementAt(1);
```

The component `JList` does not automatically provide scrolling. So, if you wish to have more choices in your list than you wish to allow space for in your GUI design you will need to provide scrolling for your list. This is quite easily done; you simply have to place your `JList` component inside a `JScrollPane` object, which automatically manages the creation of the scroll bars as necessary. The code to achieve this is given below:

```
JScrollPane scrollList = new JScrollPane(nameList);
```

The component `scrollList` is the same as the list `nameList` but now has a vertical scroll bar associated with it whenever there are more items in the list than can be displayed in the window. Details of the many features of the `JScrollPane` can be found in the Java reference documentation.

4.7 | Text fields

Text fields are used for the input of small items of textual data.

A **text field** is part of a GUI into which text can be typed by a user or which can be used to display information to the user. The `JTextField` objects are described by the class `JTextField`. These can be created using `new`. There are a number of constructors for text fields. Examples of their use are shown below:

```
JTextField txfA = new JTextField();
JTextField txfB = new JTextField(24);
JTextField txfC = new JTextField("Text Field Type here");
JTextField txfD = new JTextField("This is for typing", 20);
```

The first line creates an empty text field. The second line creates a text field that has 24 columns. The third creates a text field that contains the string "Type here". The fourth line creates a text field consisting of 20 columns with the text "This is for typing" contained in the field.

There are a number of methods associated with the JTextField class. The getText method retrieves the text that has been placed into a text field. Thus,

```
JTextField txfC = new JTextField("Text Field Type here");
String text = txfC.getText();
```

will place the string "Text Field Type here" into the string variable text. The JTextField class also contains methods that carry out actions such as retrieving text that has been highlighted by the user, selecting text depending on the start and end position of the text to be highlighted, and returning with the current length of the text field.

Calculator interface

As you saw in the calculator example, text fields can be used for output as well as for input. You are now in a position to understand the whole of the construction of the calculator interface. Although the interface has used only buttons and a text field, the approach taken would be the same with other types of components. First, design your interface on paper. Then, decide how to group the various components together onto panels that can be placed onto the frame to produce the desired effect. Using just the basic layouts that we have considered, you will be able to produce most of the designs that you are likely to need.

4.8 Text areas

A **text area** is very similar to a text field. The main difference is that a text area is capable of containing a number of lines of text, rather than the single line found in a text field. Both the class JTextArea and the class JTextField inherit from a class known as JTextComponent, which provides many of the methods that are used for manipulating objects described by these classes. Hence you will find quite a lot of commonality between the methods used for accessing and manipulating JTextArea and JTextField objects.

A text area is used for entering comparatively large amounts of textual data.

The code below creates a JTextArea object:

```
JTextArea ta = new JTextArea (4, 20);
```

It creates an empty text area that has 4 rows and 20 columns into which text is typed. The following code:

```
JTextArea ta = new
    JTextArea ("This is some text to start off with.\n" +
        "Do you like it? yes or no?", 4, 20);
```

creates a text area that is already initialized with some text.

Useful methods include getText, setText(String) and, for JTextArea, append (String). As a default, text areas have 'word wrap' switched off. It is important to point out that as with lists, text areas do not automatically scroll. The JTextArea component has to be wrapped inside a JScrollPane to enable scrolling.

4.9 | Scroll bars

Scroll bars are used to constrain the user to numerical data that lies between two limits.

A **scroll bar** is generally used as an input control element that enables a slider to be moved; when the slider is moved it transmits a value from some minimum value to a maximum value. There are a number of constructors associated with the `JScrollBar` class. The zero-argument constructor creates a scroll bar. The one-argument constructor is used to specify whether a scroll bar is to be displayed horizontally or vertically. For example:

```
JScrollBar scbV = new JScrollBar(JScrollBar.VERTICAL);
JScrollBar scbH = new JScrollBar(JScrollBar.HORIZONTAL);
```

The single argument to this constructor is one of two static constants, which can be found in the `JScrollBar` class. You will find yourself using the five-argument constructor most. The arguments for this constructor are in the following order:

1   the constant that indicates the orientation;

2   the starting position of the scroll bar;

3   the scrolling increment;

4   the minimum value to be communicated by the scroll bar;

5   the maximum value to be communicated by the scroll bar.

So, for example, the statement:

```
JScrollBar scbV = new JScrollBar
                 (JScrollBar.VERTICAL, 20, 5, 0, 80);
```

creates a vertical scroll bar that has a starting position of 20, an increment of 5, a minimum value of 0 and a maximum value of 80. When the slider in this scroll bar is moved the value is incremented or decremented in steps of 5.

A value generated by a scroll bar can be accessed by a variety of methods associated with the `JScrollBar` class. For example, the method `getValue` returns the current value of the scroll bar, `getMinimum` returns the integer that represents the minimum value of the scroll bar, `setValue` sets the value of the scroll bar and `getOrientation` returns the orientation of the scroll bar. There is also a variety of methods that alter the parameters of the scroll bar. An example of the use of the `getValue` method is shown below:

```
JScrollBar scbV = new JScrollBar
                 (JScrollBar.VERTICAL, 20, 5, 0, 80);
...
int currValue = scbV.getValue();
...
```

Here, `currValue` is updated to contain the current value of `scbV`. Figure 7 shows some of the elements described in this section being displayed in a window.

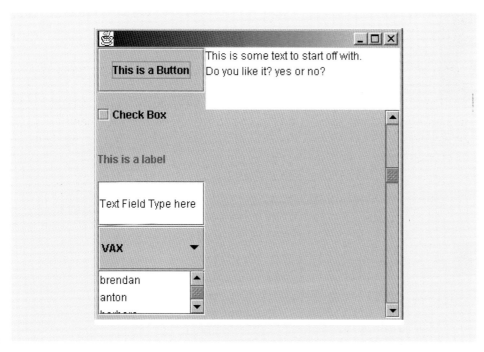

Figure 7   The visual objects that we have considered

SAQ 3

(a) In the calculator interface, buttons were used for the functions. Which other visual component could be used to allow the user to indicate the function that they wanted?

(b) Is the label on a button fixed when it is created?

(c) Why would check boxes not be a suitable alternative to buttons in part (a)?

ANSWERS ....

(a) Since only one function at a time can be selected then radio buttons could be used. A drop-down menu could also have been used. Neither of these options is suitable from an HCI point of view.

(b) No. The label on a button can be changed using the `setText` method and the current label can be retrieved using the `getText` method.

(c) With check boxes, any number of boxes can be chosen, which is not appropriate for function selection.

5 Creating user interfaces

Once you have created a container for your interface and, optionally, selected a layout manager, you can begin to add the visual components that do the real work. In this section we will illustrate some of these elements with example programs. We will also show you how inheritance can be used to build up user interfaces from existing classes that implement interface objects.

5.1 A simple class to build on

Panels can be placed in other containers.

To begin with, we introduce a class that provides the basis for adding the visual components. This class simply defines a top-level window with a number of panels, which we will use to hold examples of visual components. Remember that panels are used to group elements, such as buttons, together. Our base class for this section is as follows:

```
import java.awt.*;
import javax.swing.*;

public class SwingClass extends JFrame
{
    protected JPanel topPanel, botPanel;

    public SwingClass ()
    {
        setSize(400, 400);
        setTitle("User Interface");
        topPanel = new JPanel();
        botPanel = new JPanel();

        /* Add the elements to the frame via the contentPane. The default
        layout BorderLayout is used.*/
        Container cp = getContentPane();
        cp.add(topPanel, BorderLayout.NORTH);
        cp.add(botPanel, BorderLayout.SOUTH);
    }
}
```

To run the code we use the following class:

```
public class SwingClassTest
{
    public static void main (String[] args)
    {
        SwingClass thisClass = new SwingClass();
        thisClass.setVisible(true);
    }
}
```

Before continuing, you should read through this code in order to make sure you understand what it does. We define a new class by extending `JFrame`. We then create an instance of this class using the constructor, which carries out the process of building up the interface elements. Inside the constructor, two panels are created and then added to the frame using the `add` method. We have used this method before and glossed over the details, so it is worth providing a little more detail. Whenever you want to insert an object into a frame (or related container), you will use the `add` method. There are two ways that the method can be called. The first is the most common:

```
add(component)
```

but the second way:

```
add(component, constraint)
```

is used by layout managers (for example, the `BorderLayout` class), which use the second argument to position the component.

The `add` method you use is determined by the layout method the holder uses. If you are writing code and your calls to `add` don't seem to be working, one of the first things that you should check is whether the layout manager you are using requires a constraint argument. This is especially likely to happen with certain classes that use the `BorderLayout` class – your code will compile and run, but if you call the wrong version of `add` then the components will not appear.

5.2 Adding a menu

The first thing that we will add is a **menu bar**. This GUI element has not been described before. It is just a bar that contains menus; these, in turn, contain individual menu items. The `JMenuBar` holds `JMenus`, which in turn hold `JMenuItems`. It is the menu items that the user finally selects that cause some action to be carried out. The procedure for creating menus is somewhat long-winded. First, you must create a `JMenuBar`:

```
JMenuBar mb = new JMenuBar();
```

Then you must create a new item for each menu that is required to appear in the menu bar, for example:

```
JMenu m = new JMenu("Menu 1");
```

After this you must create a `JMenuItem` for each selectable item that is required to appear in the menu, then tell the menu to hold the item:

```
m.add(new JMenuItem("MenuItem 1"));
m.add(new JMenuItem("MenuItem 2"));
```

Once you have completed adding items to the menu, you must add the menu to the menu bar:

```
mb.add(m);
```

Finally, when all of this has been done, you must tell the frame that you want it to use the `JMenuBar` that you have prepared:

```
setJMenuBar(mb);
```

This approach is fairly straightforward and the code below shows how the menu mechanism can be incorporated within a typical frame.

The code now becomes:

```java
import java.awt.*;
import javax.swing.*;

public class SwingClass2 extends SwingClass
{
    public SwingClass2 ()
    {
        super();

        // add the menu bar and items
        JMenuBar mb = new JMenuBar();
        JMenu m = new JMenu("Menu 1");
        m.add(new JMenuItem("MenuItem 1"));
        m.add(new JMenuItem("MenuItem 2"));
        mb.add(m);
        setJMenuBar(mb);
    }
}
```

To run the code, we use the following class:

```java
public class SwingClass2Test
{
    public static void main (String[] args)
    {
        SwingClass thisClass = new SwingClass2();
        thisClass.setVisible(true);
    }
}
```

The following are a number of things to notice about this code.

1   The class `SwingClass2` extends the class `SwingClass` defined previously, so all the public and protected methods and instance variables in this class become available to `SwingClass2`.

2   The constructor in `SwingClass2` calls `super`, which in turn calls the constructor in `SwingClass`. This sets the frame and the panels previously defined.

3   The reference variable `thisClass` is declared as being of type `SwingClass` but has an object of type `SwingClass2` assigned to it. This is an example of polymorphism, because `thisClass` is expecting an instance of `SwingClass` but is actually assigned an instance of `SwingClass2` without any problems arising.

Be sure that you understand how this interface is created (see Figure 8, overleaf).

Here, we have considered only the very simplest form of menu. It is possible, for example, to have items such as `JCheckBoxMenuItem` or `JRadioButtonMenuItem` and to set mnemonic selectors.

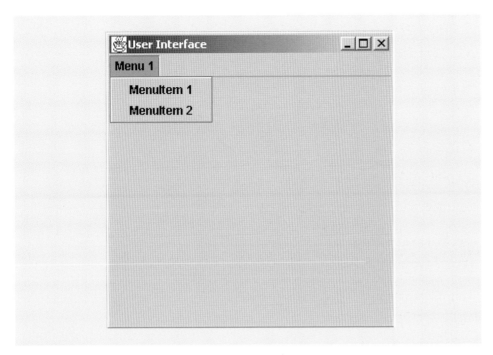

Figure 8   A window with a menu bar and menu items

5.3 Adding a text area and a drawing area

We will now continue to add some other useful elements to the top panel. We will add a text area, and an area for drawing that we will form from a JPanel component. As you will remember, a JTextArea is a general-purpose text control element that can be used to hold arbitrary text strings. We will also add scroll bars to the JTextArea.

The code to add these two elements to the display is as follows:

```
import java.awt.*;
import javax.swing.*;

public class SwingClass3 extends SwingClass2
{
    private JTextArea ta = new JTextArea("TextArea", 10, 50);

    public SwingClass3 ()
    {
        super();

        // set the layout model for the topPanel
        topPanel.setLayout(new GridLayout(1, 2));

        // create JScrollPane around JTextArea
        JScrollPane scr = new JScrollPane(ta);

        // add scrollable text area to topPanel
        topPanel.add(scr);

        // add the MyCanvas item
        topPanel.add(new MyCanvas());
    }
}
```

The code for the MyCanvas class is as follows:

```
public class MyCanvas extends JPanel
{
    public void paintComponent (Graphics g)
    {
        g.drawString("Canvas", 20, 20);
    }
}
```

and in order to display the GUI we need the following class:

```
public class SwingClass3Test
{
    public static void main (String args[])
    {
        SwingClass thisClass = new SwingClass3();
        thisClass.setVisible(true);
    }
}
```

The display from this class is shown in Figure 9.

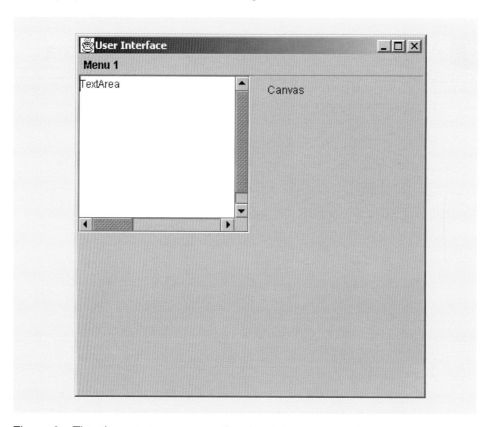

Figure 9   The class **SwingClass3** showing a text area and a canvas area

As before, we have extended the class from the previous example. In the constructor, we begin by setting the layout for the panel we will use. In this case, we initially want a grid with one row and two columns. We then employ the add method to insert a JScrollPane containing a JTextArea (with initial text set to the string "TextArea") and a MyCanvas object.

All container classes have a method for causing the components and images placed in them to appear on the screen. For a frame, this method is known as paint; for a panel, as in the example above, the method is called paintComponent. Both take an argument – a Graphics object – that enables drawing to take place. The Graphics object is supplied by the system and contains all of the methods needed for drawing on the screen. You will see more of this class and its methods in *Unit 7*. All the above code does is create a new class that inherits from JPanel and overrides the paintComponent method of JPanel with a simple instruction to display the string "Canvas" starting at (20, 20) on the panel. In the next unit, we shall describe how to *draw*, using objects defined by the Graphics class. For the moment, just assume that the MyCanvas object is an object with a simple string "Canvas" displayed on it. In *Unit 7* we will meet a related method, which containers also have: repaint. You have already made indirect use of repaint when you called setVisible to get a window to display. The method setVisible calls repaint, which calls paint and the window is then displayed on screen.

5.4   Adding other interface objects

The last set of additions to the interface will be a button, a drop-down list, a text field and a check box. This is shown in the following code:

```
import java.awt.*;
import javax.swing.*;

public class SwingClass4 extends SwingClass3
{
    public SwingClass4 ()
    {
        super();

        // add items to the botPanel
        botPanel.add(new JTextField("TextField"));
        botPanel.add(new JButton("Button"));
        botPanel.add(new JCheckBox("Checkbox"));
        JComboBox c = new JComboBox();
        c.addItem("Choice Item 1");
        c.addItem("Choice Item 2");
        c.addItem("Choice Item 3");
        botPanel.add(c);
    }
}
```

In the constructor, we simply employ the add method to insert elements into the bottom panel. Starting with the JTextField we create an instance with the default text value of "TextField". We then proceed to add a JButton, with the label on the button set to be the string "Button". We also add a JCheckBox in the same manner and then create a drop-down list using a JComboBox. Finally, the drop-down list is added to the JPanel. At this point, the interface is as shown in Figure 10.

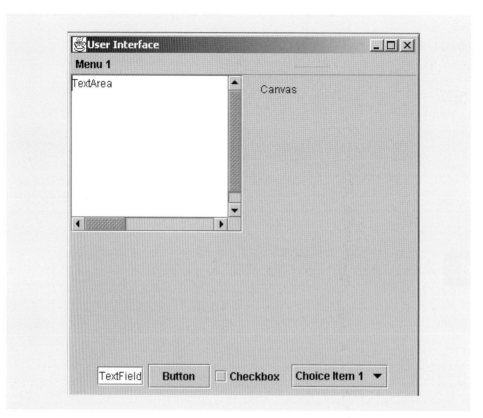

Figure 10   The class **SwingClass4** showing a range of visual components

Activity 6.4
Constructing a frame
containing a range of
Swing components.

Activity 6.5
Constructing a user
interface to demonstrate
fonts.

5.5   Visual programming

Many IDEs provide the facilities to create user interfaces using a 'drag and drop' approach from a palette of components. This approach can be highly convenient for producing quick designs. While this course will not make use of them, we would draw your attention to these features in order that you can explore them independently outside of the course.

This approach is known as **visual programming**. The IDE automatically creates the code necessary to produce the interface that you have visually created. The IDE then allows you to adjust the parameters of the components and to add the code necessary to make them work.

However, creating layouts in this way can produce code that is unnecessarily complex and may make the application less portable. As we are concerned here with teaching you programming we will not pursue this topic any further but if you have the time available, you could browse through the tutorial files included in the IDE Help option.

6   Summary

In this unit you have seen how you can create user interfaces of almost limitless complexity. We have looked at some of the more important types of GUI element that you are likely to use, including various types of buttons and a number of text components, and discussed how to make components scrollable. We also discussed how to lay out items in a window and that different layout managers are available, each of which has its own way of ordering the layout.

The components we have looked at form just a small selection of all the visual components available in the Swing classes. The number of components available, their methods and behaviours are so large that again it must be stressed that the only way to program in Java is to have the API documentation next to you, or make use of the API specification and the Java Help facility in the IDE.

However, by the end of this unit all that you are able to do is create an interface. When you click on a button or type into a text field, nothing happens. Without action, what you have created is of little use. The way in which this action is achieved is the substance of *Unit 7*, which looks at the topic of *event-driven programming*. This is a style of programming in which the program responds to events initiated by the user, such as mouse clicks and key presses.

LEARNING OUTCOMES

When you have completed this unit, you should be able to:

▶ create GUIs using a wide variety of visual components from the Java Swing package;

▶ create, lay out and show visual components;

▶ structure components within containers.

Concepts

The following concepts have been introduced in this unit:

absolute positioning, button, check box, container, drop-down list, event-driven programming, frame, graphical user interface, label, layout manager, list, menu, panel, radio button, scroll bar, Swing, text area, text field, visual component, visual programming.

Appendix 1 – calculator code

This is the complete code for the calculator developed during *Unit 6*.

```java
import java.awt.*;
import javax.swing.*;
import java.awt.event.*;

public class Calculator extends JFrame
{
    private final int NUMBER_KEY_PAD_BUTTONS = 10;
    private final int NUMBER_DIGITS = 25;

    private JButton [] keyPadButtons;
    private JButton clearButton;
    private JButton pointButton;
    private JPanel keyPadPanel;
    private JPanel displayPanel;
    private JPanel functionPanel;
    private JButton addButton;
    private JButton subtractButton;
    private JButton multiplyButton;
    private JButton divideButton;
    private JButton equalsButton;
    private JTextField displayField;
    private String currentDisplay;
    private String operand1;
    private int function;
    private double result;

    public Calculator (String title)
    {
        setSize(300, 300);
        setTitle(title);
        currentDisplay = "";

        /* Set up key pad panel containing number, CE and
        point buttons.*/
        keyPadPanel = new JPanel();
        keyPadPanel.setLayout(new GridLayout(3, 4));
        keyPadButtons = new JButton[NUMBER_KEY_PAD_BUTTONS];

        /* Create each number button, add to panel and
        add action listener.*/
        for (int i = 0; i < NUMBER_KEY_PAD_BUTTONS; i++)
        {
            keyPadButtons[i]=new JButton("" + i);
            keyPadPanel.add(keyPadButtons[i]);
            keyPadButtons[i].addActionListener(new
                          KeyPadButtonWatcher());
        }
```

```
/* Create CE and point button, add to panel and add
action listener.*/
clearButton = new JButton("CE");
pointButton = new JButton(".");
keyPadPanel.add(clearButton);
keyPadPanel.add(pointButton);
clearButton.addActionListener(new KeyPadButtonWatcher());
pointButton.addActionListener(new KeyPadButtonWatcher());

// set up display field panel
displayPanel = new JPanel();
displayField = new JTextField(NUMBER_DIGITS);
displayField.setText("0.0");
displayPanel.add(displayField);

// create function panel and function buttons
functionPanel = new JPanel();
functionPanel.setLayout(new GridLayout(5, 1));
addButton = new JButton("+");
subtractButton = new JButton("-");
multiplyButton = new JButton("*");
divideButton = new JButton("/");
equalsButton = new JButton("=");

// add function buttons to panel
functionPanel.add(addButton);
functionPanel.add(subtractButton);
functionPanel.add(multiplyButton);
functionPanel.add(divideButton);
functionPanel.add(equalsButton);

// add action listeners to function buttons
addButton.addActionListener(new FunctionButtonWatcher());
subtractButton.addActionListener(new FunctionButtonWatcher());
multiplyButton.addActionListener(new FunctionButtonWatcher());
divideButton.addActionListener(new FunctionButtonWatcher());
equalsButton.addActionListener(new EqualsButtonWatcher());

// add functionality to close icon
setDefaultCloseOperation(JFrame.EXIT_ON_CLOSE);

// get content pane and add panels to frame
Container cp = getContentPane();
cp.add(displayPanel,BorderLayout.NORTH);
cp.add(keyPadPanel,BorderLayout.CENTER);
cp.add(functionPanel,BorderLayout.EAST);
}
```

```java
private class KeyPadButtonWatcher implements ActionListener
{
    public void actionPerformed (ActionEvent a)
    {
        Object buttonPressed = a.getSource();
        if (buttonPressed.equals(keyPadButtons[0]))
        {
            currentDisplay = currentDisplay + "0";
            displayField.setText(currentDisplay);
        }

        if (buttonPressed.equals(keyPadButtons[1]))
        {
            currentDisplay = currentDisplay + "1";
            displayField.setText(currentDisplay);
        }

        if (buttonPressed.equals(keyPadButtons[2]))
        {
            currentDisplay = currentDisplay + "2";
            displayField.setText(currentDisplay);
        }

        if (buttonPressed.equals(keyPadButtons[3]))
        {
            currentDisplay = currentDisplay + "3";
            displayField.setText(currentDisplay);
        }

        if (buttonPressed.equals(keyPadButtons[4]))
        {
            currentDisplay = currentDisplay + "4";
            displayField.setText(currentDisplay);
        }

        if (buttonPressed.equals(keyPadButtons[5]))
        {
            currentDisplay = currentDisplay + "5";
            displayField.setText(currentDisplay);
        }

        if (buttonPressed.equals(keyPadButtons[6]))
        {
            currentDisplay = currentDisplay + "6";
            displayField.setText(currentDisplay);
        }

        if (buttonPressed.equals(keyPadButtons[7]))
        {
            currentDisplay = currentDisplay + "7";
            displayField.setText(currentDisplay);
        }
```

```
        if (buttonPressed.equals(keyPadButtons[8]))
        {
           currentDisplay = currentDisplay + "8";
           displayField.setText(currentDisplay);
        }

        if (buttonPressed.equals(keyPadButtons[9]))
        {
           currentDisplay = currentDisplay + "9";
           displayField.setText(currentDisplay);
        }

        if (buttonPressed.equals(pointButton))
        {
           currentDisplay = currentDisplay + ".";
           displayField.setText(currentDisplay);
        }

        if (buttonPressed.equals(clearButton))
        {
           currentDisplay = "";
           displayField.setText("0.0");
        }
     }
  }

  private class FunctionButtonWatcher implements ActionListener
  {
     public void actionPerformed (ActionEvent a)
     {
        Object buttonPressed = a.getSource();
        if (buttonPressed.equals(addButton))
        {
           operand1 = currentDisplay;
           function = 1;
           currentDisplay = "";
           displayField.setText(currentDisplay);
        }

        if (buttonPressed.equals(subtractButton))
        {
           operand1 = currentDisplay;
           function = 2;
           currentDisplay = "";
           displayField.setText(currentDisplay);
        }

        if (buttonPressed.equals(multiplyButton))
        {
           operand1 = currentDisplay;
           function = 3;
           currentDisplay = "";
           displayField.setText(currentDisplay);
        }
```

```java
        if (buttonPressed.equals(divideButton))
        {
            operand1 = currentDisplay;
            function = 4;
            currentDisplay = "";
            displayField.setText(currentDisplay);
        }
    }
}

private class EqualsButtonWatcher implements ActionListener
{
    public void actionPerformed (ActionEvent a)
    {
        switch (function)
        {
            case 1:
            {
                result = Double.parseDouble(operand1) +
                        Double.parseDouble(currentDisplay);
                displayField.setText("" + result);
                break;
            }
            case 2:
            {
                result = Double.parseDouble(operand1)-
                        Double.parseDouble(currentDisplay);
                displayField.setText("" + result);
                break;
            }
            case 3:
            {
                result = Double.parseDouble(operand1) *
                        Double.parseDouble(currentDisplay);
                displayField.setText("" + result);
                break;
            }
            case 4:
            {
                result = Double.parseDouble(operand1) /
                        Double.parseDouble(currentDisplay);
                displayField.setText("" + result);
            }
        }
    }
}
}
```

To create an object of type `Calculator` and run the code we use the class `RunningExampleTest` as follows:

```
public class RunningExampleTest
{
    public static void main (String[] args)
    {
        Calculator fd = new Calculator("Calculator Example");
        fd.setVisible(true);
    }
}
```

Index

A
absolute positioning 16
Abstract Windowing Toolkit 6
AWT 6, 21

B
BorderLayout 12, 29
buttons 11–12, 21, 33
    ButtonGroup 23
    JButton 12
    radio buttons 22

C
check boxes 22
combo box 23
constructors, super 30
containers 6, 9–11
    JFrame 9
    panels 9

D
drag and drop 34
drop-down lists 23, 33

E
event-driven programming 7

F
FlowLayout 14

G
graphical user interface 5
Graphics 33

GridLayout 15–16, 32
GUI 5, 21

J
JButton 12, 33
JCheckBox 22
JComboBox 23, 33
JFrame 6, 9, 29
JLabel 22
JList 24
JMenuBar 29
JMenuItems 29
JPanel 9, 14, 28, 31, 33
JRadioButton 23
JScrollBar 26
JScrollPane 24
JTextArea 25, 31
JTextField 24–25, 33

L
label 22
layout 10
    absolute positioning 16
    BorderLayout 12, 29
    FlowLayout 14
    GridLayout 15–16, 31
    layout managers 6, 16, 29
    LayoutManager 11

lists 24
    drop-down lists 23, 33
    JList 24
    scrolling 24

M
menu bar 29

P
paint 32
panels 6, 9, 28, 31, 33
polymorphism 30
portability 6, 34

R
radio buttons 22

S
scrolling 24
    JScrollPane 24
    scroll bars 26, 31
super 30
Swing 21
    hierarchy 7
    library 6

T
text area 25
text field 24–25, 33

V
visual components 6, 11
visual programming 34